A Shake and a Shiver

Written by Larry Dane Brimner • Illustrated by JoAnn Adinolfi

Published in the United States of America by The Child's World®
PO Box 326 • Chanhassen, MN 55317-0326
800-599-READ • www.childsworld.com

Reading Adviser

Cecilia Minden-Cupp, PhD, Director of Language and Literacy, Harvard University Graduate School
of Education, Cambridge, Massachusetts

Acknowledgments

The Child's World®: Mary Berendes, Publishing Director

Editorial Directions, Inc.: E. Russell Primm, Editorial Director and Project Manager; Katie Marsico,
Associate Editor; Judith Shiffer, Assistant Editor; Matt Messbarger, Editorial Assistant

The Design Lab: Kathleen Petelinsek, Design and art production

Library of Congress Cataloging-in-Publication Data

Brimner, Larry Dane.
  A shake and a shiver / written by Larry Dane Brimner ; illustrated by JoAnn Adinolfi.
    p. cm. — (Magic door to learning)
  Summary: Carson learns the difference between hot and cold while piling on more and more
winter clothes.
  ISBN 1-59296-531-8 (lib. bdg. : alk. paper) [1. Cold—Fiction. 2. Clothing and dress—Fiction.]
1. Adinolfi, JoAnn, ill. II. Title.
  PZ7.B767Sha 2005
  [E]—dc22   2005005366

A book is a door, a magic door.
It can take you places
you have never been before.
Ready? Set?
Turn the page.
Open the door.
Now it is time to explore.

"I'm cold," said Carson.

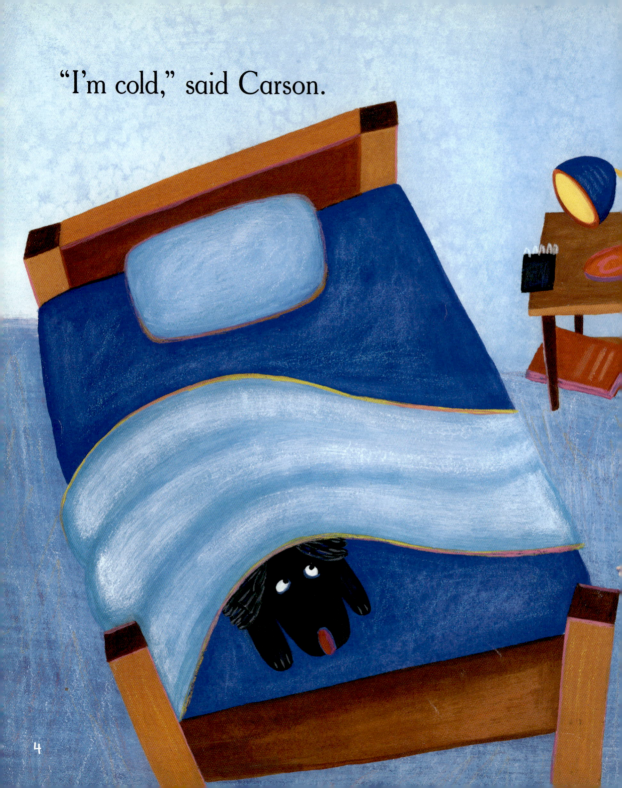

Mama knew what to do. She gave Carson some warm socks and furry boots for his feet. Papa knew what to do. He helped Carson pull a woolly sweater over his shirt.

"Brrrrr," said Carson with a shake and a shiver. "I'm still cold."

8

His sister Cassidy knew
what to do. She brought
Carson a cap to wear
on his head. Uncle Leo
knew what to do. He
gave Carson a mug of
steaming hot chocolate.

Carson hugged his arms together.
"I'm still cold," he chattered.

Auntie Maria knew what
to do. She brought Carson
a long, heavy jacket. It
reached all the way down
to the cuffs of his pants.
Grandmother knew what to
do. She wrapped a muffler
around Carson's neck.

"Are you warm yet?" she asked.

Carson shook his head.
"Not yet," he said.

His cousin Amanda knew
what to do. She gave
Carson some mittens
for his hands. His other
cousin Jill knew what to do.
She gave Carson a pair of
earmuffs to warm his ears.

19

20

Grandfather knew
what to do. He
wrapped Carson up
in a cozy blanket
so that only his eyes
and nose peeked out.

"I'm hot!" said Carson.
And he knew just
what to do.

Our story is over, but there is still much to explore beyond the magic door!

How do you stay cozy and warm when it's cold outside? The next time it's chilly, ask an adult to help you make hot chocolate. Prepare enough to share with your whole family. Before serving, add some marshmallows and whipped cream to your taste treat!

These books will help you explore at the library and at home:

Colandro, Lucille, and Jared Lee (illustrator). *There Was a Cold Lady Who Swallowed Some Snow!* New York: Scholastic, 2003.

Rylant, Cynthia, and Sucie Stevenson (illustrator). *Henry and Mudge Get the Cold Shivers.* New York: Bradbury Press, 1989.

About the Author

Larry Dane Brimner is an award-winning author of more than 120 books for children. When he isn't at his computer writing, he can be found biking in Colorado or hiking in Arizona. You can visit him online at *www.brimner.com.*

About the Illustrator

JoAnn Adinolfi lives in New Hampshire, a place where it gets really cold in the winter. So, she does a lot of shaking and shivering herself. Making books keeps her warm, as does her favorite orange hat!